Welcome

The special features of
to develop and recall r
mathematical facts.

Some of the special features are –

- hints to help with the learning of facts
- special flap on the book to make learning easy
- follow-up activities to reinforce the facts
- interesting information associated with the facts
- in line with the Revised Mathematics Curriculum – tables do not exceed the 10 fact e.g. 4+10, 4x10
- 4 pages about the Euro!
- addition and subtraction tables are on opposite pages to focus on subtraction as the inverse of addition.
- multiplication and division tables are on opposite pages to focus on division as the inverse of multiplication.

We hope that you enjoy using **Time for Tables**!

First published 2002
The Educational Company of Ireland
Ballymount Road,
Walkinstown,
Dublin 12.
A trading unit of Smurfit Ireland Ltd.

09S15

© The author
Artwork: Niamh Jackman
Design and layout: Graham &
Stapleton Design Consultants

CONTENTS

Addition
and
Subtraction
Tables

Hints to help you with your + and − tables

- Use concrete materials, (cubes, counters, links, conkers, matchsticks, etc.) to construct your tables.

- Look for the tables with the 🗝 symbol.
  - **doubles**; 2 + 2, 3 + 3 etc.
  - **facts of 10**; 6 + 4, 7 + 3 etc.
  - **adding to 10s**; 1 + 10, 2 + 10 etc.

- Look for
  - **near doubles**; 2 + 3, 3 + 4 etc.
  - **near facts of 10**; 6 + 5, 7 + 4 etc.
  - **adding to 9s**; (one less than adding to 10s).

- Look for **twice known facts...**
  Remember that the order of numbers in your addition tables does not matter
  4 + 3 = 7
  3 + 4 = 7

- Remember that **subtraction is inverse addition**
  4 + 3 = 7
  7 − 3 = 4
  7 − 4 = 3

Learning your tables

- **Look** at the tables carefully and **say** each fact at least three times.

- When you think that you know the tables, **cover** the answers with the special flaps on the covers of this book.

- Say the tables without looking at the answers.

- Ask someone to listen to you saying the tables.

- **Write** the tables, keeping the answers covered.

- **Check** your answers.

- Think of ways to help you to remember the tables you find difficult e.g. birthdays, ages, house numbers, digits in telephone and car registration numbers.

- Share your ideas with others!

After you have learned your tables

- Write or say the activities where you see these symbols 🖊 or 💬

- Think of and do other activities.

- Read the information facts associated with the tables where you see this symbol ⓘ

- Answer the questions where you see this symbol ❓

- Think of other facts that you would associate with the tables.

- Revise your tables frequently.

  and...

- Remember to use the tables you have learnt when you are doing your maths!

0+

0	+	0	=	0
0	+	1	=	1
0	+	2	=	2
0	+	3	=	3
0	+	4	=	4
0	+	5	=	5
0	+	6	=	6
0	+	7	=	7
0	+	8	=	8
0	+	9	=	9
0	+	10	=	10

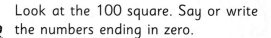

Look at the 100 square. Say or write the numbers ending in zero.

−0

0	−	0	=	0
1	−	0	=	1
2	−	0	=	2
3	−	0	=	3
4	−	0	=	4
5	−	0	=	5
6	−	0	=	6
7	−	0	=	7
8	−	0	=	8
9	−	0	=	9
10	−	0	=	10

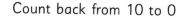

Count back from 10 to 0

1+

1	+	0	=	1
1	+	1	=	2
1	+	2	=	3
1	+	3	=	4
1	+	4	=	5
1	+	5	=	6
1	+	6	=	7
1	+	7	=	8
1	+	8	=	9
1	+	9	=	10
1	+	10	=	11

Count in ones from 10 to 30.

−1

1	−	1	=	0
2	−	1	=	1
3	−	1	=	2
4	−	1	=	3
5	−	1	=	4
6	−	1	=	5
7	−	1	=	6
8	−	1	=	7
9	−	1	=	8
10	−	1	=	9
11	−	1	=	10

SUBTRACTION

Count back in ones from 25 to 0

2+

	2	+	0	=	2
	2	+	1	=	3
🗝	2	+	2	=	4
	2	+	3	=	5
	2	+	4	=	6
	2	+	5	=	7
	2	+	6	=	8
	2	+	7	=	9
🗝	2	+	8	=	10
	2	+	9	=	11
🗝	2	+	10	=	12

ⓘ A pair is two of a kind.

✎ Write the tables in your copy.

−2

2	−	2	=	0
3	−	2	=	1
4	−	2	=	2
5	−	2	=	3
6	−	2	=	4
7	−	2	=	5
8	−	2	=	6
9	−	2	=	7
10	−	2	=	8
11	−	2	=	9
12	−	2	=	10

SUBTRACTION

(i) There are two kinds of elephants – African and Indian.

3+

3	+	0	=	3
3	+	1	=	4
3	+	2	=	5
3	+	3	=	6
3	+	4	=	7
3	+	5	=	8
3	+	6	=	9
3	+	7	=	10
3	+	8	=	11
3	+	9	=	12
3	+	10	=	13

(i) A triangle has three sides.

Write out the tables that you found most difficult to learn.

14

−3

$$3 - 3 = 0$$
$$4 - 3 = 1$$
$$5 - 3 = 2$$
$$6 - 3 = 3$$
$$7 - 3 = 4$$
$$8 - 3 = 5$$
$$9 - 3 = 6$$
$$10 - 3 = 7$$
$$11 - 3 = 8$$
$$12 - 3 = 9$$
$$13 - 3 = 10$$

SUBTRACTION

ⓘ A shamrock has three leaves.

4	+	0	=	4
4	+	1	=	5
4	+	2	=	6
4	+	3	=	7
4	+	4	=	8
4	+	5	=	9
4	+	6	=	10
4	+	7	=	11
4	+	8	=	12
4	+	9	=	13
4	+	10	=	14

ADDITION

(i) A square has four equal sides.

 Write the tables that have answers more than 10.

16

−4

4	−	4	=	0
5	−	4	=	1
6	−	4	=	2
7	−	4	=	3
8	−	4	=	4
9	−	4	=	5
10	−	4	=	6
11	−	4	=	7
12	−	4	=	8
13	−	4	=	9
14	−	4	=	10

 Name the four seasons of the year.

5+

5	+	0	=	5
5	+	1	=	6
5	+	2	=	7
5	+	3	=	8
5	+	4	=	9
5	+	5	=	10
5	+	6	=	11
5	+	7	=	12
5	+	8	=	13
5	+	9	=	14
5	+	10	=	15

(i) There are five vowels in the English language: a,e,i,o,u.

Write the tables that have answers less than 10.

−5

5	− 5	=	0
6	− 5	=	1
7	− 5	=	2
8	− 5	=	3
9	− 5	=	4
10	− 5	=	5
11	− 5	=	6
12	− 5	=	7
13	− 5	=	8
14	− 5	=	9
15	− 5	=	10

SUBTRACTION

(?) Have a tables quiz with your group.
Take turns asking the tables.

6+

6	+ 0	=	6
6	+ 1	=	7
6	+ 2	=	8
6	+ 3	=	9
6	+ 4	=	10
6	+ 5	=	11
6	+ 6	=	12
6	+ 7	=	13
6	+ 8	=	14
6	+ 9	=	15
6	+ 10	=	16

(i) Insects have six legs.

Write the tables, putting the numbers in a different order: Example: 0 + 6 = 6

20

−6

6	− 6	=	0
7	− 6	=	1
8	− 6	=	2
9	− 6	=	3
10	− 6	=	4
11	− 6	=	5
12	− 6	=	6
13	− 6	=	7
14	− 6	=	8
15	− 6	=	9
16	− 6	=	10

(i) Six is half of a dozen.

7+

7	+	0	=	7
7	+	1	=	8
7	+	2	=	9
7	+	3	=	10
7	+	4	=	11
7	+	5	=	12
7	+	6	=	13
7	+	7	=	14
7	+	8	=	15
7	+	9	=	16
7	+	10	=	17

ⓘ There are seven colours in the rainbow.

💬 Can you name them?

22

−7

7	− 7	=	0
8	− 7	=	1
9	− 7	=	2
10	− 7	=	3
11	− 7	=	4
12	− 7	=	5
13	− 7	=	6
14	− 7	=	7
15	− 7	=	8
16	− 7	=	9
17	− 7	=	10

SUBTRACTION

(?) How many dwarfs are in the story about Snow White?

8+

8	+	0	=	8
8	+	1	=	9
8	+	2	=	10
8	+	3	=	11
8	+	4	=	12
8	+	5	=	13
8	+	6	=	14
8	+	7	=	15
8	+	8	=	16
8	+	9	=	17
8	+	10	=	18

(i) A spider has eight legs.

Write out 4 pairs of tables.
Example 8 + 6 = 14; 14 – 8 = 6.

24

−8

8	−	8	=	0
9	−	8	=	1
10	−	8	=	2
11	−	8	=	3
12	−	8	=	4
13	−	8	=	5
14	−	8	=	6
15	−	8	=	7
16	−	8	=	8
17	−	8	=	9
18	−	8	=	10

(?) Have a quiz with your group on 7+, −7, 8+, −8 tables. Take turns asking the tables.

9+

	9	+	0	=	9
🔑	9	+	1	=	10
	9	+	2	=	11
	9	+	3	=	12
	9	+	4	=	13
	9	+	5	=	14
	9	+	6	=	15
	9	+	7	=	16
	9	+	8	=	17
🔑	9	+	9	=	18
🔑	9	+	10	=	19

Write the tables that you found most difficult to learn.

−9

9	−	9	=	0
10	−	9	=	1
11	−	9	=	2
12	−	9	=	3
13	−	9	=	4
14	−	9	=	5
15	−	9	=	6
16	−	9	=	7
17	−	9	=	8
18	−	9	=	9
19	−	9	=	10

Write the tables that have answers more than 5.

10+

	10	+	0	=	10
	10	+	1	=	11
	10	+	2	=	12
	10	+	3	=	13
	10	+	4	=	14
	10	+	5	=	15
	10	+	6	=	16
	10	+	7	=	17
	10	+	8	=	18
	10	+	9	=	19
	10	+	10	=	20

ⓘ There are 10 years in a decade.

 Write the tables that have answers more than 15.

−10

10	− 10	=	0
11	− 10	=	1
12	− 10	=	2
13	− 10	=	3
14	− 10	=	4
15	− 10	=	5
16	− 10	=	6
17	− 10	=	7
18	− 10	=	8
19	− 10	=	9
20	− 10	=	10

Write 5 pairs of tables.
Example: 10 + 2 = 12; 12 − 10 = 2.

Multiplication and Division Tables

Hints to help you with your x and ÷ tables

- Remember that multiplication is repeated addition.

- Remember that division is repeated subtraction.

- Use concrete materials, (cubes, counters, links, conkers, matchsticks, etc.) to construct your tables.

- Practice skip counting (counting in multiples) forward and backwards.

- Use 100 squares and colour in the multiples.

- Look for the tables with the 🔑 symbol.
  - **doubles**; 2 x 2, 3 x 3 etc.
  - **tens**; 10 x 2, 10 x 3 etc.

- Look for
  - **near doubles**, one set more or one set less
  - **near tens**

- Look for the **twice known facts** because... the order of the numbers in multiplication tables does not matter e.g. $4 \times 3 = 12$; $3 \times 4 = 12$.

- Remember that **division is inverse multiplication**. $4 \times 3 = 12$; $12 \div 3 = 4$; $12 \div 4 = 3$ (except for 0 tables).

- Look for **number patterns** e.g.
  – all of the answers in multiplication tables, 2, 4, 6, 8 and 10 are even numbers
  – all of the answers in multiplication tables 5 end in 5 or 0.
  – all of the answers in multiplication tables 10 end in 0.

- Use the 100 square and colour in the patterns.

- Read pages 6 and 7 again... and you will be ready to start your multiplication and division tables!

x0

0	x	0	=	0
1	x	0	=	0
2	x	0	=	0
3	x	0	=	0
4	x	0	=	0
5	x	0	=	0
6	x	0	=	0
7	x	0	=	0
8	x	0	=	0
9	x	0	=	0
10	x	0	=	0

MULTIPLICATION

ⓘ 0° is freezing point on the Celcius temperature scale.

0÷

0	÷	1	=	0
0	÷	2	=	0
0	÷	3	=	0
0	÷	4	=	0
0	÷	5	=	0
0	÷	6	=	0
0	÷	7	=	0
0	÷	8	=	0
0	÷	9	=	0
0	÷	10	=	0

DIVISION

ⓘ The latitude of the equator is zero degrees (0°).

x1

0	x	1	=	0
1	x	1	=	1
2	x	1	=	2
3	x	1	=	3
4	x	1	=	4
5	x	1	=	5
6	x	1	=	6
7	x	1	=	7
8	x	1	=	8
9	x	1	=	9
10	x	1	=	10

(i) A unit is one thing.
January 1st is New Year's Day in many countries.

÷1

0	÷	1	=	0
1	÷	1	=	1
2	÷	1	=	2
3	÷	1	=	3
4	÷	1	=	4
5	÷	1	=	5
6	÷	1	=	6
7	÷	1	=	7
8	÷	1	=	8
9	÷	1	=	9
10	÷	1	=	10

DIVISION

ⓘ A Cyclops has one eye.
The Titanic sank on its first voyage.

x2

0	x	2	=	0
1	x	2	=	2
2	x	2	=	4
3	x	2	=	6
4	x	2	=	8
5	x	2	=	10
6	x	2	=	12
7	x	2	=	14
8	x	2	=	16
9	x	2	=	18
10	x	2	=	20

ⓘ The tide ebbs and flows twice a day.

 Write the tables with even numbered answers.

38

÷2

0	÷	2	=	0
2	÷	2	=	1
4	÷	2	=	2
6	÷	2	=	3
8	÷	2	=	4
10	÷	2	=	5
12	÷	2	=	6
14	÷	2	=	7
16	÷	2	=	8
18	÷	2	=	9
20	÷	2	=	10

DIVISION

(i) K2 (Mount Godwin Austen) is the second highest mountain in the world.

x3

0	x	3	=	0
1	x	3	=	3
2	x	3	=	6
3	x	3	=	9
4	x	3	=	12
5	x	3	=	15
6	x	3	=	18
7	x	3	=	21
8	x	3	=	24
9	x	3	=	27
10	x	3	=	30

(i) A goal in Gaelic Football is equal to 3 points.

 Write the tables that have odd numbered answers.

÷3

$$0 \div 3 = 0$$
$$3 \div 3 = 1$$
$$6 \div 3 = 2$$
$$9 \div 3 = 3$$
$$12 \div 3 = 4$$
$$15 \div 3 = 5$$
$$18 \div 3 = 6$$
$$21 \div 3 = 7$$
$$24 \div 3 = 8$$
$$27 \div 3 = 9$$
$$30 \div 3 = 10$$

(i) There are three months in each season of the year.
Name the three months of spring.

x4

0	x	4	=	0
1	x	4	=	4
2	x	4	=	8
3	x	4	=	12
4	x	4	=	16
5	x	4	=	20
6	x	4	=	24
7	x	4	=	28
8	x	4	=	32
9	x	4	=	36
10	x	4	=	40

 Name the four suits in a deck of cards.

 Write the tables that you found difficult to learn.

÷4

0	÷	4	=	0
4	÷	4	=	1
8	÷	4	=	2
12	÷	4	=	3
16	÷	4	=	4
20	÷	4	=	5
24	÷	4	=	6
28	÷	4	=	7
32	÷	4	=	8
36	÷	4	=	9
40	÷	4	=	10

DIVISION

(i) A quadruped is a four-footed animal.

x5

0	**x**	**5**	**=**	**0**
1	**x**	**5**	**=**	**5**
2	**x**	**5**	**=**	**10**
3	**x**	**5**	**=**	**15**
4	**x**	**5**	**=**	**20**
5	**x**	**5**	**=**	**25**
6	**x**	**5**	**=**	**30**
7	**x**	**5**	**=**	**35**
8	**x**	**5**	**=**	**40**
9	**x**	**5**	**=**	**45**
10	**x**	**5**	**=**	**50**

MULTIPLICATION

(i) There are 50 states in the U.S.A.

Write the tables with answers ending in 5.

÷5

0	÷	5	=	0
5	÷	5	=	1
10	÷	5	=	2
15	÷	5	=	3
20	÷	5	=	4
25	÷	5	=	5
30	÷	5	=	6
35	÷	5	=	7
40	÷	5	=	8
45	÷	5	=	9
50	÷	5	=	10

DIVISION

(?) December 25th is Christmas Day.
Have a quiz with your group on the x
and ÷ tables that you have learned.

x6

0	x	6	=	0
1	x	6	=	6
2	x	6	=	12
3	x	6	=	18
4	x	6	=	24
5	x	6	=	30
6	x	6	=	36
7	x	6	=	42
8	x	6	=	48
9	x	6	=	54
10	x	6	=	60

(i) A hexagon is a six-sided figure.

 Write the tables with answers more than 30.

÷6

0	÷	6	=	0
6	÷	6	=	1
12	÷	6	=	2
18	÷	6	=	3
24	÷	6	=	4
30	÷	6	=	5
36	÷	6	=	6
42	÷	6	=	7
48	÷	6	=	8
54	÷	6	=	9
60	÷	6	=	10

DIVISION

Count in 6s from 60 to 120.

x7

0	x	7	=	0
1	x	7	=	7
2	x	7	=	14
3	x	7	=	21
4	x	7	=	28
5	x	7	=	35
6	x	7	=	42
7	x	7	=	49
8	x	7	=	56
9	x	7	=	63
10	x	7	=	70

MULTIPLICATION

(i) There are seven bones in the human neck.

(i) The opposite sides of a dice add up to seven.

÷7

0	÷	7	=	0
7	÷	7	=	1
14	÷	7	=	2
21	÷	7	=	3
28	÷	7	=	4
35	÷	7	=	5
42	÷	7	=	6
49	÷	7	=	7
56	÷	7	=	8
63	÷	7	=	9
70	÷	7	=	10

DIVISION

Write down 5 pairs of tables.
Example: 7 x 4 = 28; 28 ÷ 7 = 4

x8

0	x	8	=	0
1	x	8	=	8
2	x	8	=	16
3	x	8	=	24
4	x	8	=	32
5	x	8	=	40
6	x	8	=	48
7	x	8	=	56
8	x	8	=	64
9	x	8	=	72
10	x	8	=	80

(i) A chess or draughts board has 64 squares.

 Write the tables, putting the numbers in a different order. Example: 8 x 0 = 0

50

÷8

0	÷	8	=	0
8	÷	8	=	1
16	÷	8	=	2
24	÷	8	=	3
32	÷	8	=	4
40	÷	8	=	5
48	÷	8	=	6
56	÷	8	=	7
64	÷	8	=	8
72	÷	8	=	9
80	÷	8	=	10

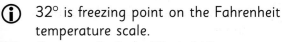 32° is freezing point on the Fahrenheit temperature scale.
Count in 8s from 80 to 160.

x9

0	x	9	=	0
1	x	9	=	9
2	x	9	=	18
3	x	9	=	27
4	x	9	=	36
5	x	9	=	45
6	x	9	=	54
7	x	9	=	63
8	x	9	=	72
9	x	9	=	81
10	x	9	=	90

 Name the nine counties of Ulster.

 Add the digits in the answers and comment on the result.

÷9

0	÷	9	=	0
9	÷	9	=	1
18	÷	9	=	2
27	÷	9	=	3
36	÷	9	=	4
45	÷	9	=	5
54	÷	9	=	6
63	÷	9	=	7
72	÷	9	=	8
81	÷	9	=	9
90	÷	9	=	10

DIVISION

ⓘ A right angle is an angle of 90°.

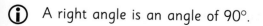 Count back in nines from 180 to 90.

x10

0	x	10	=	0
1	x	10	=	10
2	x	10	=	20
3	x	10	=	30
4	x	10	=	40
5	x	10	=	50
6	x	10	=	60
7	x	10	=	70
8	x	10	=	80
9	x	10	=	90
10	x	10	=	100

(i) A century is 100 years.

(?) What century are we living in?

÷10

0	÷ 10	=	0
10	÷ 10	=	1
20	÷ 10	=	2
30	÷ 10	=	3
40	÷ 10	=	4
50	÷ 10	=	5
60	÷ 10	=	6
70	÷ 10	=	7
80	÷ 10	=	8
90	÷ 10	=	9
100	÷ 10	=	10

DIVISION

(?) Have a group quiz on your x and ÷ tables.

The Metric System

The metric system for measurement was created by a group of French scientists in the 1790's.

Length

unit = 1 metre

10 millimetres (mm) = 1 centimetre (cm)
10 centimetres (cm) = 1 decimetre (dm)
10 decimetres (dm) = 1 METRE (m)
10 metres (m) = 1 decametre (dam)
10 decametres (dam) = 1 hectometre (hm)
10 hectometres (hm) = 1 kilometre (km)

Quick facts

10 millimetres (mm) = 1 centimetre (cm)
100 centimetres (cm) = 1 METRE (m)
1 000 metres = 1 kilometre (km)

Did you know ...

- that the Nile (the longest river in the world) is 6 670 km?
- that the Great Wall of China (the longest wall in the world) is 3 460 km?

Weight
unit = 1 gramme

10 milligrammes (mg) = 1 centigramme (cg)
10 centigrammes (cg) = 1 decigramme (dg)
10 decigrammes (dg) = 1 GRAMME (g)
10 grammes (g) = 1 decagramme (dag)
10 decagrammes (dag) = 1 hectogramme (hg)
10 hectogrammes (hg) = 1 kilogramme (kg)
1 000 kilogrammes (kg) = 1 tonne (t)

Quick facts
1 000 milligrammes (mg) = 1 gramme (g)
1 000 grammes (g) = 1 kilogramme (kg)
1 000 kilogrammes (kg) = 1 tonne (t)

Did you know …
- that the St Bernard is one of the heaviest breeds of domestic dog? A male dog can weigh up to 91 kg.
- that some dinosaurs weighed 120 tonnes?

Capacity

unit = 1 litre

10 millilitres (ml) = 1 centilitre (cl)
10 centilitres (cl) = 1 decilitre (dl)
10 decilitres (dl) = 1 LITRE (l)
10 litres (l) = 1 decalitre (dal)
10 decalitres (dal) = 1 hectolitre (hl)
10 hectolitres (hl) = 1 kilolitre (kl)

Quick fact
1 000 millilitres (ml) = 1 litre (l)

Did you know …
- that every person uses about 260 litres of water a day?
- that it takes up to 110 litres of water to run a washing machine?
- that we use at least 19 litres of water for every minute that we spend in the shower?
- that 1 litre of water weighs 1kg?

Area

unit = 1 are

10 centiares (ca) = 1 deciare (da)
10 deciares (da) = 1 ARE (a)
10 ares (a) = 1 decare (daa)
10 decares (daa) = 1 hectare (ha)

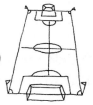

Quick fact

100 ares (a) = 1 hectare (ha)

Did you know ...

- that the largest vineyard in the world is in France? It covers an area of 840 000 hectares.
- that the base of the Great Pyramid in Egypt covers 5 hectares?

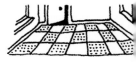

Square Measure

100 sq.millimetres = 1 sq.centimetre
  ($100mm^2 = 1cm^2$)

100 sq.centimetres = 1 sq.decimetre
  ($100cm^2 = 1dm^2$)

100 sq.decimetres = 1 sq.meter
  ($100dm^2 = 1m^2$)

100 sq.metres = 1 sq.decametre
  ($100m^2 = 1\ dam^2$)

100 sq.decametres = 1 sq.hectometre
  ($100\ dam^2 = 1\ hm^2$)

100 sq.hectometres = 1 sq.kilometre
  ($100\ hm^2 = 1\ km^2$)

Quick fact

$1\,000\,000\ m^2 = 1\ km^2$
  ($100\ m^2 = 1\ are$)

Did you know ...

- that the Sahara desert is about
  $9\,269\,000\ km^2$?
- that the Vatican City (the smallest
  country in the world) is only $0.44km^2$?

60

Temperature

Temperature is measured by an instrument called a thermometer.

Fahrenheit scale

212° Water boils

104° Warm water

98° Normal body temperature

68° A warm day

32° Freezing point

Celsius scale

100° Water boils

40° Warm water

37° Normal body temperature

20° A warm day

0° Freezing point

Did you know ...

● A German named Fahrenheit and a Swedish astronomer named Anders Celsius devised the temperature scales?

The Euro €

The Euro is the currency of the 19 shaded countries. The Euro was introduced on the 1st January 2002. € is the euro symbol.

There are 7 euro notes.

5 euro

10 euro

20 euro

50 euro

100 euro

200 euro

500 euro

Euro notes look the same both front and back in the twelve countries.

Euro coins

There are **8 euro** coins

1 euro = 100 cent

The front of the euro coins looks the same in the twelve countries but ...

the reverse side of the coins has a
national design.

Ireland	France	Spain
Germany	Italy	Belgium
Netherlands	Greece	Portugal
Austria	Luxembourg	Finland

All euro notes and coins circulate freely
within the twelve countries.

Other currencies

Britain: £1 Sterling = 100 pence
Denmark: 1 Krone = 100 öre
Sweden: 1 Krona = 100 öre
Switzerland: 1 Swiss Franc = 100 centimes

U.S.A.: 1 Dollar ($) = 100 cents
Canada: 1 Dollar = 100 cents
Australia: 1 Dollar = 100 cents
Japan: 1 Yen = 100 sen
Russia: 1 Ruble = 100 kopecks
Turkey: 1 Turkish Lira = 100 kuras
Egypt: 1 pound = 100 piastes
Mexico: 1 Peso = 100 centaros
China: 1 Yuan = 100 fen

Roman numerals

The Romans used letters instead of figures when writing numbers.

1	=	I	16	=	XVI
2	=	II	17	=	XVII
3	=	III	18	=	XVIII
4	=	IV	19	=	XIX
5	=	V	20	=	XX
6	=	VI	30	=	XXX
7	=	VII	40	=	XL
8	=	VIII	50	=	L
9	=	IX	60	=	LX
10	=	X	70	=	LXX
11	=	XI	80	=	LXXX
12	=	XII	90	=	XC
13	=	XIII	100	=	C
14	=	XIV	500	=	D
15	=	XV	1 000	=	M

Angles

Right angle
(angle of 90°)

Acute angle
(less than 90°)

Obtuse angle
(more than 90°)

Straight line angle
(angle of 180°)

Reflex angle
(more than 180°)

4 right angles = 1 full circle
= 360°.

Shapes

Triangle
A triangle is a shape with
3 lines and 3 angles.

Equilateral triangle
All sides and all angles are equal.

Isosceles triangle
Two sides are equal and their
opposite angles are equal.

Scalene triangle
Three unequal sides and three
unequal angles.

Right-angled triangle
One of the angles is a right angle.

Quadrilaterals

A quadrilateral is a shape with four lines and four angles.

Square
All sides are equal and all angles are right angles.

Rectangle
Opposite sides are equal and all angles are right angles.

Rhombus
All sides are equal, opposite sides are parallel and opposite angles are equal.

Parallelogram
Opposite sides are equal and parallel. Opposite angles are equal.

Trapezium
One pair of opposite sides are parallel but not equal.

Other shapes

Polygon
A polygon is a figure with many angles and sides.

Pentagon
5 equal sides
5 equal angles

Hexagon
6 equal sides
6 equal angles

Octagon
8 equal sides
8 equal angles

Circle
Every point on a circle is equal distance from the centre point
r = radius, d = diameter.

SHAPES

3-D shapes

Cube

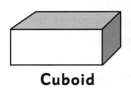

Cuboid

Pyramid

Triangular Prism

Cone

Cylinder

Sphere

SOLIDS

Lines

Vertical lines
Line A is a vertical line

Horizontal lines
Line B is a horizontal line.

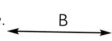

Diagonal
A diagonal often joins one corner of a shape to the opposite corner.
C is a diagonal

Parallel lines
Parallel lines go in the same direction and are always the same distance apart.
Lines D and E are parallel lines.

Perpendicular lines
A vertical line is perpendicular to the horizontal line and is at right angles to it. Line F is perpendicular to line H.

Time

60 seconds = 1 minute
60 minutes = 1 hour
24 hours = 1 day
7 days = 1 week
52 weeks = 1 year
365 days = 1 year
366 days = 1 leap year.

Days in months

28 days: February
29 days: February in a leap year
30 days: April, June, September,
November
31 days: January, March, May, July,
August, October, December.

A time rhyme

Thirty days hath September,
April, June and November.
All the rest have thirty-one
But February, twenty-eight alone
Except in Leap year, once in four
February has one day more.

Did you know ...

- that the Tour de France cycle race lasts for three weeks?
- that the Olympic games are held every four years?
- that a powered model aircraft flew for 33 hrs, 30 min, 15 sec in the U.S.A. in October 1992?

The 12-hour clock
am – pm

am = the period between midnight and noon
pm = the period between noon and midnight.

7 am = 7 o'clock in the morning.

11 pm = 11 o'clock at night

Did you know …
● that the longest day of the year in the
Northern hemisphere is June 21st and that
the shortest day is December 21st?

The 24-hour clock

The twenty-four-hour clock runs straight through from midnight to midnight. Four figures are always used in writing the time on a twenty-four-hour clock.

12.00 midnight	=	00.00 hours
1.00 am	=	01.00 hours
3.00 am	=	03.00 hours
12.00 noon	=	12.00 hours
1.00 pm	=	13.00 hours
3.00 pm	=	15.00 hours

Did you know ...
● that at 12 noon in Ireland, it is 7 am in New York, but it is 9 pm in Tokyo?

Fractions

Fractions	Decimal Fractions	Percentages
$\frac{1}{10}$	0.1	10%
$\frac{2}{10}$	0.2	20%
$\frac{3}{10}$	0.3	30%
$\frac{4}{10}$	0.4	40%
$\frac{5}{10}$	0.5	50%
$\frac{6}{10}$	0.6	60%
$\frac{7}{10}$	0.7	70%
$\frac{8}{10}$	0.8	80%
$\frac{9}{10}$	0.9	90%
$\frac{10}{10}$	1	100%

FRACTIONS

Fractions

Fractions	Decimal Fractions	Percentages
$\frac{1}{2}$	0.5	50%
$\frac{1}{4}$	0.25	25%
$\frac{3}{4}$	0.75	75%
$\frac{1}{5}$	0.2	20%
$\frac{2}{5}$	0.4	40%
$\frac{3}{5}$	0.6	60%
$\frac{4}{5}$	0.8	80%
$\frac{1}{8}$	0.125	$12\frac{1}{2}\%$
$\frac{3}{8}$	0.375	$37\frac{1}{2}\%$
$\frac{5}{8}$	0.625	$62\frac{1}{2}\%$
$\frac{7}{8}$	0.875	$87\frac{1}{2}\%$
$\frac{1}{3}$	0.333	$33\frac{1}{3}\%$
$\frac{2}{3}$	0.666	$66\frac{2}{3}\%$
$\frac{1}{100}$	0.01	1%

Symbols used in mathematics

+ plus or addition

− minus or subtraction

x multiplication

÷ division

= is equal to

≠ is not equal to

> is greater than

≯ is not greater than

< is less than

≮ is not less than

∠ angle   **△** triangle

□ square   **○** circle

|| parallel to   **⊥** perpendicular to

Did you know ...

the + and − symbols were first published in Germany in 1489 by John Wideman?